1

Claire Buckley has been a teacher and textile designer for 20 years, teaching in secondary schools as well as exhibiting her work in galleries. She is the Chairman of the Young Embroiderers Guild. Her designs use embroidery for fashion and accessories and she often uses recycled materials. Her projects for children have been featured in magazines as well as on the internet. Her hobbies include yoga, travelling to interesting places and shopping for shoes.

Other titles in this series:

Start to Quilt
Miriam Edwards

Start to Knit
Alison Dupernex

Start to Embroider
Claire Buckley

Start to Bead
Jill Thomas

Start to
Embroider

SEARCH PRESS

First published in Great Britain 2007
Search Press Ltd.
Wellwood
North Farm Road
Tunbridge Wells
Kent TN2 3DR

Photographs by Steve Crispe at Search Press Studios and by Roddy Paine Photographic Studios.

ISBN-10: 1-84448-111-5
ISBN-13: 978-1-84448-111-8

Suppliers
If you have difficulty obtaining any of the materials and equipment mentioned in this book, please visit the Search Press website for details of suppliers:
www.searchpress.com

Some words are underlined <u>like this</u>. They are explained in the glossary on page 48.

To my students, past, present and future, who constantly challenge me and inspire me to be creative.

Acknowledgements

I would like to thank the following people for their help, support and encouragement while creating this book: Dorothy Tucker, Education Officer of the Embroiderers' Guild; Roz, Edd and Steve at Search Press; my family, friends and colleagues, and especially my students, who have tested the projects and offered many positive ideas and comments.

The publishers would like to thank consultant Rebecca Vickers; and also Katherine Chandrain, Katrina Hindley, Lucia Brisefer, Nicole Fields and Charlie de la Bédoyère for appearing in the photographs.

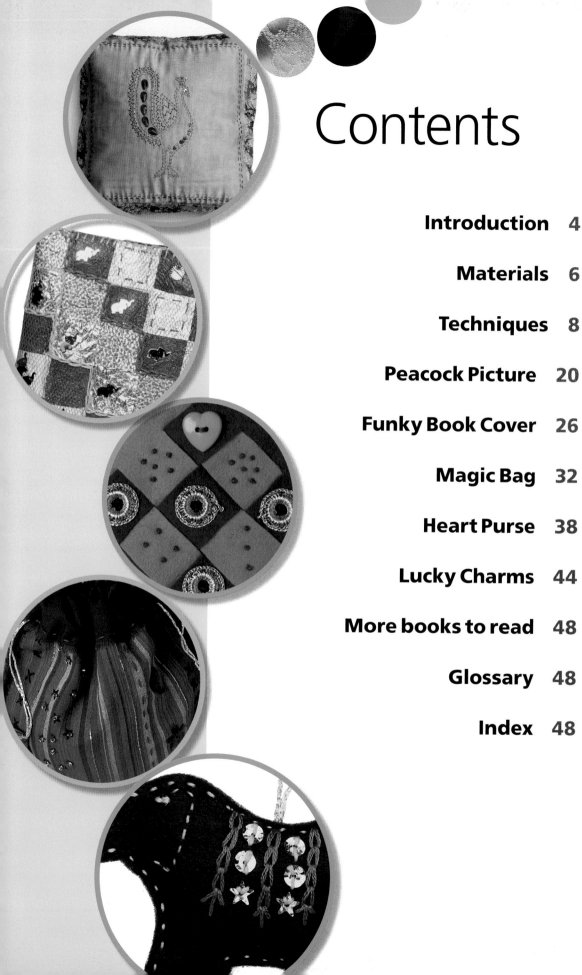

Contents

Introduction

Embroidery is the wonderful craft in which fabrics are decorated with stitches, beads, sequins and other fabrics. This book will show you everything you need to start to embroider.

People have been creating fabulous effects on fabrics with embroidery for many thousands of years. The basic techniques have not altered, but fashions in embroidery – such as the way that we use colour, patterns and stitches – change over time, much like fashions in clothing.

Some of the Funky Facts tell you where the words that we use in embroidery come from, and this helps us to understand the history and origins of embroidery.

We can get lots of ideas for our embroidery by looking at embroideries from other countries and periods of time. Embroideries made in India are very inspirational in the way that they use colours, patterns and materials.

For each project you will find the basic instructions as well as tips on how to improve your embroidery and ideas for other things you could make. If you already know some of the basics, the book will help you to do even more exciting work with fabrics and threads.

FUNKY FACT!

Lots of the words that we use in embroidery come from France in the Middle Ages. This is possibly because when the Normans conquered England in 1066, the new French court brought their embroidery and language to England.

This bag from India uses mirrors (or sheesha), shells and metal, as well as stitches and beads to cover almost the entire surface of the fabric with decorations.

Glass beads are used to brighten the tassels on the corners of the bag. The bag is made from a square of fabric which is folded in like an envelope. The top flap is fastened by the cord being wrapped around the bag.

You should enjoy many happy hours creating wonderful embroideries for yourself, your family and your friends. There is nothing better than being able to say 'I made this'!

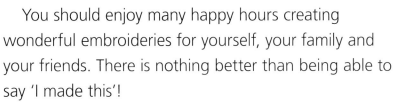

TOP TIP!

Try keeping a sketchbook in which you can collect all of your embroidery ideas by making drawings or sticking in exciting pictures, fabrics and other things you find in your everyday life.

Materials

Fabrics

You can use many different fabrics in your embroidery. These include **cotton**, **felt** and **denim**, as well as more unusual fabrics like **calico**, a firm woven cotton fabric which can be bought unbleached or bleached white; **cotton lawn**, a very soft, finely-woven cotton fabric; **organza**, a thin, stiff and <u>translucent</u> woven fabric which can be made from silk or synthetic fibres; **net**, an open mesh fabric used in layers over other fabrics to add colour and strength; and **brocade**, a rich fabric often made of silk woven with a raised pattern.

Many fabrics come striped, spotted, dyed in different colours, or printed with designs, so there will always be a fabric that you like.

Threads and yarns

Threads and yarns are used to pick out designs on the fabrics, and this is the essence of embroidery. **Stranded embroidery thread** (called six-strand embroidery floss in the US) is used for most embroidery, and is made up of six thin strands. It is bought in a <u>skein</u>, and the thread is usually pulled apart into three strands before you start to embroider.

In addition to stranded embroidery thread, you can use **perle cotton thread** (called pearl cotton in the US). This comes in a ball and is twisted together, meaning that you do not need to split the thread before embroidering. You can also use **metallic threads**, which are useful to <u>couch</u> on to a fabric, (see page 14) or for handles and decorations.

Ribbons and **cords** (tightly twisted thread-like ropes) are both used for bag handles and decorations.

Other equipment

Large scissors These are used to cut fabrics into shape.

Embroidery scissors Smaller scissors with a sharp point, used to cut threads, cords and ribbons.

Needles For embroidery you need to have a needle with a long eye so that the thread goes into the eye easily.

Tapestry needle Tapestry needles are very large, and used for embroidering with thick threads. They are also known as ballpoint needles.

Pins These are used to hold fabrics in place or to mark where you need to sew.

Pincushion You can get many different kinds of pincushion. They are used to store pins safely and ready to use.

Safety pins These metal pins can be fixed to the end of a ribbon to pull it through a drawstring bag. See the Magic Bag project (pages 32–35) for details of how this is done.

Pencil and ruler Used for measuring fabric and thread.

Polyester wadding Used to fill the Lucky Charms (page 34). It is called 'batting' in the US.

Tambour ring A tambour ring (also known as an embroidery ring; or an embroidery hoop in the US) is used to hold fabric tight for embroidering.

Bias binding A narrow strip of fabric used to wrap around the inner ring of a tambour ring to protect the fabric when it is pulled tight.

Glue stick This is used to hold chocolate wrappers in place before they are stitched on securely in the Funky Book Cover project on pages 26–29.

Sequins Small shiny shapes that can be sewn on to fabric for decoration.

Beads Glass, metal or plastic shapes with a hole through the centre. Thread is passed through the hole to secure the bead to the fabric.

Craft jewels These are shiny plastic shapes that look like real jewels, and are used for decorating your embroidery.

Buttons These make good decorations, as well as being useful to secure bags.

Chocolate wrappers These are used in the Funky Book Cover project for decoration.

FUNKY FACT!
Many people collect equipment used for embroidery. Sometimes really old pieces can be rare and valuable.

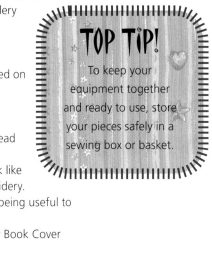

TOP TIP!
To keep your equipment together and ready to use, store your pieces safely in a sewing box or basket.

Techniques

It is important to learn these basic techniques to get your embroidery off to a good start. When you have mastered the basics, you can go on to use more complicated techniques with different fabrics and stitches.

❋ Framing up

Many fabrics are too soft to stitch without being held tight in an embroidery frame. The most commonly used frame is the tambour ring. This is made of two wooden rings. The inner ring has to be covered with bias binding so that the fabric is not damaged when the outer ring is fixed over the inner ring, which holds the fabric tight.

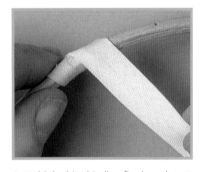

1 Hold the bias binding firmly and start to wrap the inner hoop, taking care to overlap the previously laid section of binding as shown.

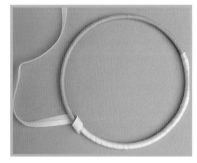

2 Continue wrapping the binding all the way around the hoop, making sure to keep the binding tight as you go.

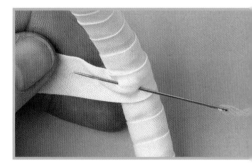

3 Thread your needle with stranded embroidery thread. Take the needle through the binding where it overlaps your starting point.

4 Take the needle through the binding again. This secures the binding with a 'back stitch'.

5 Place the covered ring flat on a table and lay the fabric right side up on top of the ring.

6 Place the outer ring of the frame on top of the fabric and inner ring. Tighten the screw fastener and pull the fabric until it is tight.

Preparing your thread and threading a needle

This is very easy to do. Lots of people use needle-threading gadgets, but you can simply hold the needle still in one hand and put the end of the thread into the eye of the needle.

1 Hold the label of the skein and pull the end of the thread until the thread reaches from your hand to your elbow, and cut it.

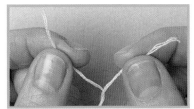

2 The thread is made of six strands and you need three strands to stitch. Divide the thread into two groups of three strands and pull them apart carefully.

3 Hold the needle still in one hand, flatten the end of the thread with your lips and push this through the eye of the needle.

 # Starting off

To hold the thread in place in the fabric, you need to sew a small 'back stitch' before you start to embroider.

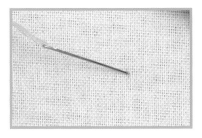

1 Push the needle through the fabric from the back. Pull the thread through, leaving a 1cm (½in) tail at the back of the fabric.

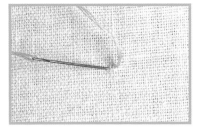

2 On the front of the fabric, push the needle back into the fabric close to where it came up. Pull the thread through tightly.

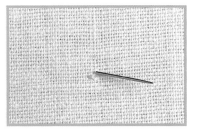

3 Now push the needle through to the front again where it first came up. Pull to tighten the stitch firmly. You are now ready to embroider!

 # Finishing off

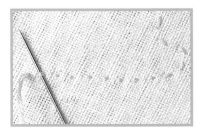

1 On the back of the fabric, push the needle through one of the stitches near the end of your stitching.

2 Pull the thread gently until it forms a loop, then push the needle into the loop and pull the thread through.

3 Pull the thread tight to hold the stitches, then cut off the excess thread leaving a 1cm (½in) end.

9

Stitches

✳ Running stitch

Running stitch is the most simple and useful stitch to learn.
It just goes up and down through the fabric.

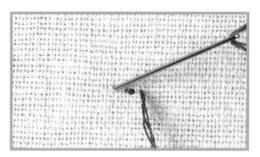
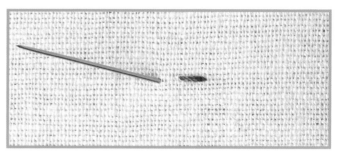

I Start off by making a back stitch (see page 8).
Bring the needle up through the fabric to the right
of the back stitch, and then back down to the left of
the back stitch.

2 As you pull the thread tight, the back stitch
will be covered neatly as shown. Working
from right to left, bring the needle back up
through the fabric and repeat.

TOP TIP!

If you are left-handed,
work from left to
right, rather than
right to left.

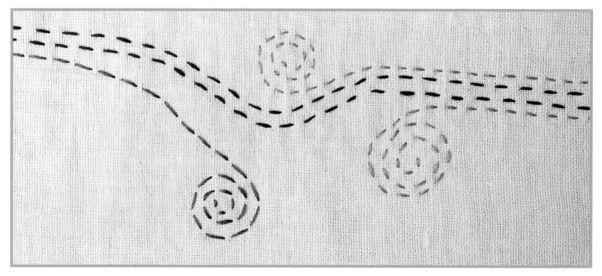

A completed row of running stitch.

*Running stitch is so simple, but it can be used to make
all sorts of attractive designs.*

Chain stitch

Chain stitch is made up of interlocking loops or chains on the right side of the fabric.

I Make a back stitch, then bring the needle up through the fabric. Hold the loop of thread in place with your thumb, and pass the needle down next to the back stitch.

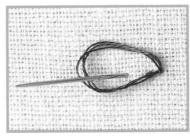

2 Bring the needle up through the loop.

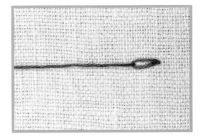

3 Gently tighten the loop by pulling the thread tight.

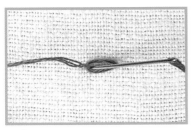

4 Start the next stitch by passing the needle down inside the loop of the last one.

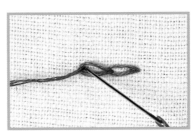

5 Repeat steps 2–4 until the chain is as long as you need it.

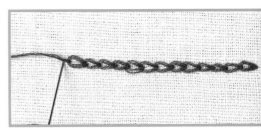

6 Finish off your row with a small stitch to fix the thread.

A completed row of chain stitch.

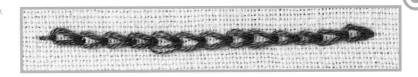

Chain stitch can be used to make attractive designs as well as basic lines.

✳ Fly stitch

Fly stitch is like a single chain stitch, but the loop is not closed or fixed at one point. This makes the stitch very useful because you can change the length of each part of the 'Y' shape. Try to overlap the stitches for a decorative effect, or stitch in rings to make stars.

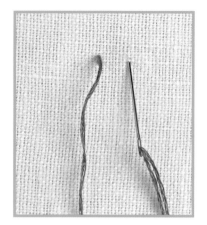

1 Bring the needle up through the fabric, then back down, creating an open loop, which lies towards you.

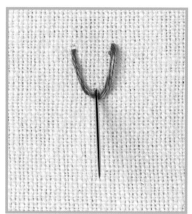

2 Bring the needle back up through the fabric, creating a 'V' shaped loop.

3 Bring the needle over the 'V' shape and down through the fabric, pulling the thread tight.

TOP TIP!

It is easiest to work fly stitch sideways from right to left.

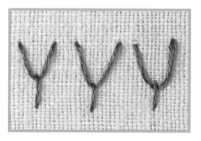

4 Start the next stitch to the left of the last one.

A completed row of fly stitch.

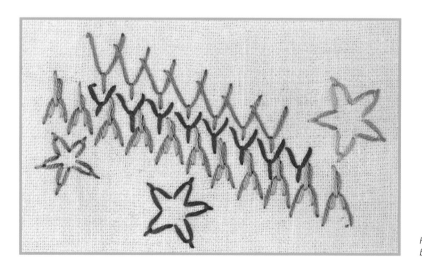

Fly stitch can be interlocked to create beautiful patterns.

Blanket stitch

This is called blanket stitch as it is used to neaten the edges of blankets. For a more decorative effect, try overlapping the stitches in different lengths and colours.

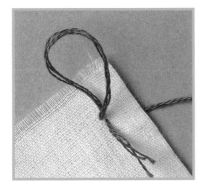

1 On the back of the fabric near the edge, make a back stitch to start off the thread. With the back of the fabric still facing you, put the needle back through to create a loop as shown.

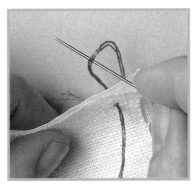

2 Turn the fabric over, and take the needle through the loop.

3 Gently tug the thread to close the loop. This will anchor the end of the row of stitches.

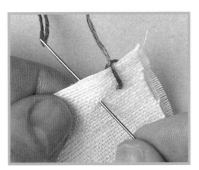

4 Pull the needle through the fabric to create a loop.

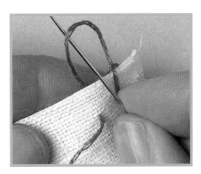

5 Put the needle back through the loop at the edge of the fabric.

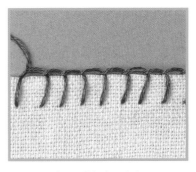

A completed row of blanket stitch.

TOP TiP!

This stitch is brilliant to add a decorative edge to pieces of fabric.

Blanket stitch looks good when overlapped in different lengths and colours.

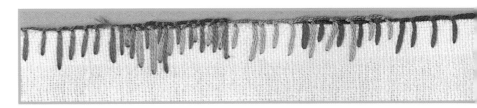

✳ Cross stitch

Cross stitch can be used singly, in lines, or in groups to make your design. Vary the size and shape of your cross stitches. For example, imagine a four-sided shape and fit the stitch across the shape from corner to corner.

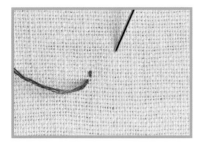

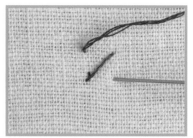

1 Start the thread off with a back stitch, then bring the needle up at the bottom left point and push the needle in at the top right point.

2 Take the thread across the back and come up at the top left point, go across the front and down at the bottom right.

3 Pull the thread until an 'x' is made. This is the first stitch. Push the needle up again ready for the next stitch.

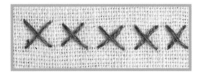

A completed row of cross stitch.

✳ Couching

Couching is used when you want to use a thread that is too thick to go easily through your fabric, so it is laid on top and held in place by small stitches – often in a different colour. You should start by taking the end of the couching thread through to the back of the fabric to make it neat and fix it in place.

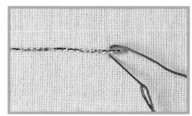

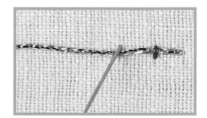

1 Thread a tapestry needle with the thick couching thread. From the front of the fabric push the needle into the fabric where you want to start couching. Remove the tapestry needle.

2 Use a thin thread with an embroidery needle to make small stitches over the couching thread.

3 Continue stitching along the length of the couching thread. At the end re-thread the couching thread on the tapestry needle and push it to the back of the work to neaten the threads, fasten with the thin thread.

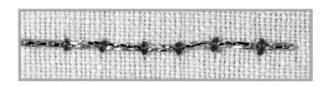

A completely couched thread.

✳ French knots

French knots can be used to add texture and detail to your embroidery.

1 Start by making a back stitch, then bring the needle up and wrap the thread around the needle.

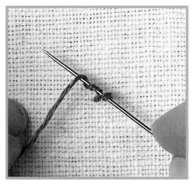

2 Continue wrapping the thread around the needle to form a spiral. The more times you wrap the thread around, the bigger the final knot.

3 Push the needle back through the fabric near where you came up and pull the thread through to create the knot.

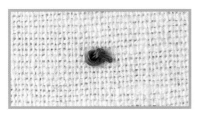

A completed French knot.

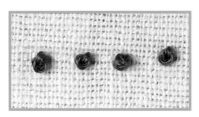

A row of French knots.

FUNKY FACT!

In France a 'French knot' is called *le point de noeud*. This means 'the spot where the knot is'.

TOP TIP!

Do not worry if the knots do not all come out looking tight. The loose texture can look as good as tight knots on your work.

A flower made up of different-coloured French knots.

Embellishments

This is where the fun really starts with your embroidery. You can go mad adding all sorts of decorations (called embellishments) to make your embroidery really personal. Look out for unusual sequins, beads and buttons in shops.

Sequins

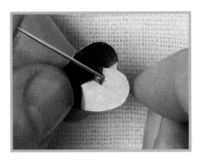

1 Thread your needle and bring it up through the fabric and through the hole in the centre of the sequin.

2 Place the sequin where you want it and take the needle through the fabric at the top of the sequin.

3 Fix the sequin by pulling the thread tight. Finish off or continue sewing on sequins in your design.

Beads

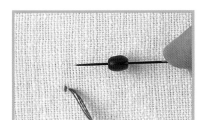  

1 Make a back stitch, then bring your threaded needle up through the fabric and put the bead on to it.

2 Push the needle back through the fabric close to where you came up, and pull the thread tight.

3 This will fix the bead in place. Carry on adding beads this way to make your design.

Sequin and bead combination

It is fun to hold sequins in place with a bead. Try to experiment with different sizes and colours of beads and sequins.

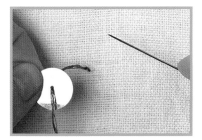 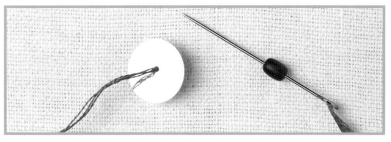

1 Place the sequin where you want it to sit, and bring your threaded needle up through the centre of the sequin.

2 Pick up the bead on to the needle. You might like to use more than one bead.

There are hundreds of different designs of beads and sequins you can use.

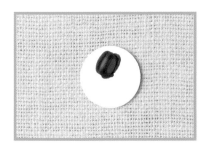

3 Push the needle back through the centre of the sequin and pull the thread gently to tighten.

✺ Buttons

Buttons are very easy to sew on to fabric, and make great simple decorations for embroidered pieces. To attach the buttons very firmly, simply sew them on with two or three stitches rather than one.

Two-hole buttons

1 Thread the needle as usual, then place the button and come up through one of the holes. Put the needle in the second hole.

2 Take the needle down through the second hole, pull the thread to hold the button in place and fasten off as usual.

Four-hole buttons

To sew four-hole buttons on, it is fun to do a cross stitch as it makes it look more interesting.

1 Place the button, and bring your threaded needle up through the bottom left hole and down through the top right hole.

2 Bring the needle up through the top left hole and down through the bottom right hole. Fasten off at the back as usual.

The button sewn on with a cross stitch.

Mock sheesha

Sheesha is the Hindi word for 'mirror' and comes from the Persian for 'fragment'. It can also be spelt *shisha*. Sheesha are usually small round mirrors, but they can also be square, as seen on the bag on page 4. When the sun shines on the mirror, the bright reflection gives the illusion that the embroidery has expensive jewels on it.

Mock sheesha are made of two parts, a plastic ring covered with coloured stitches and a round silver disc like a sequin without a hole.

1 Anchor the ring with a small stitch, then start to sew the ring in place with neat running stitches through the coloured stitches of the ring.

2 When you are halfway round, slide the silver disc under the ring.

3 Carry on stitching until you have gone the whole way round, then knot the thread at the back of the fabric to secure it.

Silver mock sheesha and craft jewels. The jewels are sewn on like sequins.

Peacock Picture

You will need

HB pencil

White cotton lawn, 30cm (12in) square

Turquoise cotton, 30cm (12in) square

Turquoise/rust organza, 30cm (12in) square

20cm (8in) tambour ring

Embroidery needle

Stranded embroidery threads in blue, green and purple

Five craft jewels

Thick gold thread

Tapestry needle

Sequins

Pins

Two 10cm (4in) lengths of narrow ribbon

Embroidered pictures are a great way to decorate your room and show off your embroidery skills. This lovely picture is inspired by designs from India. It uses some of the basic techniques with stitches, sequins and craft jewels and has loops so that you can hang it on your wall.

TOP TIP!

The white cotton lawn is placed behind the top fabrics to support and add strength to your embroidery, as the stitches and jewels can get quite heavy.

The pattern for the Peacock Picture, reproduced at actual size.

1 Trace the pattern directly on to the turquoise cotton lawn fabric, using the HB pencil.

2 Layer the three fabrics with the white cotton lawn at the back, turquoise cotton in the middle and the organza on the top. Hold them together with a pin.

3 Put the fabrics into the tambour ring, ensuring that the design is in the centre. Remember to pull the fabrics tight!

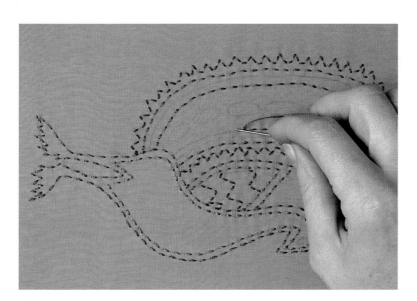

4 Thread your needle with the blue embroidery thread and outline the design with running stitch. Keep the stitches quite small and regular to ensure that the peacock looks neat. Once the blue outline is completed, use the green and purple threads to add running stitch details as shown.

5 The running stitch completed.

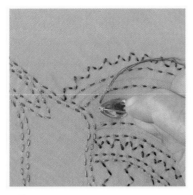

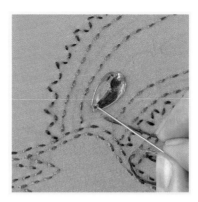

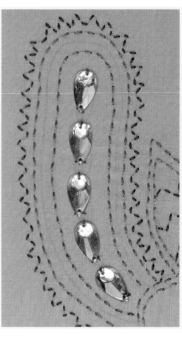

6 Attach the first craft jewel on to the tail through the bottom hole, following the instructions for attaching sequins on page 16. Do not fasten off the thread yet.

7 Secure the jewel by coming up through the fabric and back down through the hole at the bottom of the craft jewel. Tie off the end of the thread at the back of the fabric.

8 Take the thread through the top of the craft jewel to finish, then sew on the other jewels, as shown, until the tail is complete.

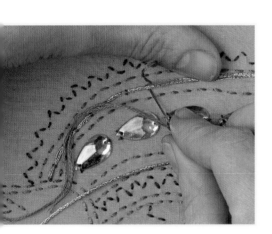

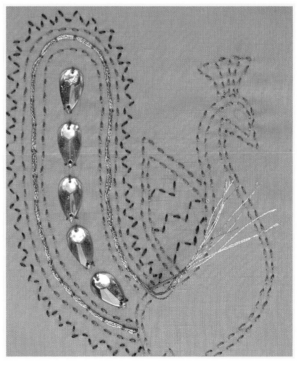

9 Place the gold thread on the tapestry needle, bring it up through the tail and lay it down, following the line. Thread the embroidery needle with purple thread and couch the gold thread all the way along, following the instructions on page 14.

10 Once you have finished couching, re-thread the gold thread on the tapestry needle and take it through the fabric. Remove the needle and tie off the gold thread at the back.

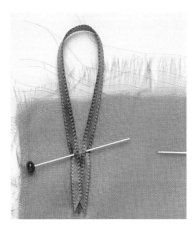

11 Sew the sequins on to the peacock's body, eye and the crown of the head, as shown above, following the instructions on page 16.

12 Remove the embroidery from the tambour ring. Secure the edges with pins. This holds the three layers of fabric in place so that you can sew the edges.

13 At each of the top corners of the fabric, pin a loop of ribbon.

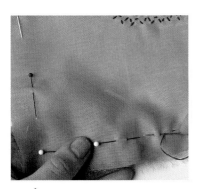

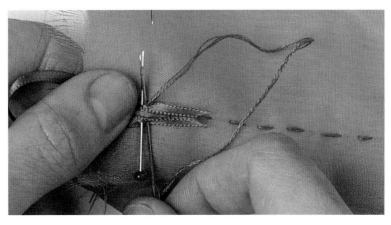

14 Start to stitch the edge using running stitch, removing the pins as you get to them.

15 Fix the ribbons in place with a small back stitch as you get to them.

TOP TIP!

You could easily use one of your own designs for an embroidered picture.

16 Continue stitching the edges, removing the pins as you go.

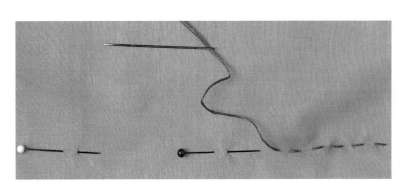

The finished Peacock Picture.

What next?

The ideas here show how the design can easily be changed.

Try using different sequins and jewels on the body, tail and edges.

You could also use a different design of a peacock to make a pair of wall hangings, or use couching on the edges as well as in the design.

Make a cushion from the embroidery by using a fabric that looks good with the embroidered picture.

Funky Book Cover

If you like chocolates then you will love collecting the wrappers for this project. The shiny foils and plastic wrappers are perfect to make this beautiful, colourful book cover. This project is quick to make and would be perfect as a present for your family or friends.

You will need

- White cotton calico
- Orange netting
- Blue coloured cotton for the lining
- Notebook
- Chocolate wrappers
- Large scissors
- Glue stick
- Embroidery needle
- Stranded embroidery threads in blue, red and yellow
- Elephant and circle sequins
- Blue ribbon and star button for the bookmark

1. Cut the white cotton calico, netting and coloured cotton to the same size as your opened notebook plus a 1cm (½in) border at the top and bottom, and a 4cm (1½in) border on each side.

2. Cut the wrappers into small squares. Make sure that the squares are all the same size.

TOP TiP!
You could use photographs or postage stamps in place of the wrappers to make the project more personal.

3. Lay out the wrappers into your design and attach them to the white cotton calico using the glue stick.

4 Continue sticking the wrappers on to the white cotton calico.

5 Lay the net over the wrappers and fabric and pin it on. The net protects the wrappers from being knocked off or damaged.

6 Work chain stitch diagonally across the cover in a stepped shape round the squares as shown. Use three different coloured threads. This will secure the netting to the fabric.

7 Work running stitch within some of the squares for decoration and extra strength. Again, vary the colours of the threads you use.

8 Sew on the sequins. Round and elephant-shaped sequins have been used here, but you could use any sort of sequin that you want.

You should now have a cover that looks like this.

9 Turn the book cover over and pin the blue cotton lining on to it.

10 Trim the excess fabric off the sides of the book cover with a pair of large scissors.

11 Edge both of the short ends with blanket stitch.

Detail of the stitching and decorations.

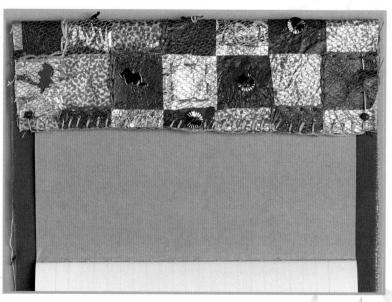

12 Put the notebook inside the cover and fold the excess fabric over the book's covers; making sure you have equal amounts of the fabric on both sides.

13 Remove the notebook and use blanket stitch to secure the long edges as shown. Stitch a length of ribbon into the centre of the top edge to make the bookmark.

14 Put the notebook into the cover and tie a small star button to the ribbon.

The finished Funky Book Cover.

What next?

Add buttons and cut wrappers into the shape of your initials to personalise your book cover.

A large sketchbook is useful to collect all of your design ideas, so make a beautiful cover. This one has chocolate coin wrappers with sequins (in lots of different shapes and sizes); beads and fly stitch in circles; and an extra large button on the bookmark.

Use the wrappers and cross stitch to make the spine of the book stand out. Attach a red foil heart to make a perfect present.

Magic Bag

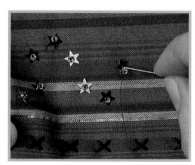

This magic bag will fool everyone until they know the secret of how to open it using the handles. You pull one set to close the bag and the other set to open it. You can also use your imagination and the other techniques in the book to add extra decoration to the bag and the handles.

Place the smaller rectangle in the middle of the larger rectangle and use a pin to hold them together.

TOP TIP!

To get the lovely frayed edges for the bag, tear the fabric to the correct size. Do this by measuring the fabric, making a small cut in the edge and then tearing the fabric.

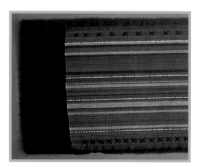

2 Thread the needle with purple embroidery thread, and sew the two rectangles together using cross stitches on the long sides of the smaller rectangle as shown.

3 Add sequins with beads to build your design.

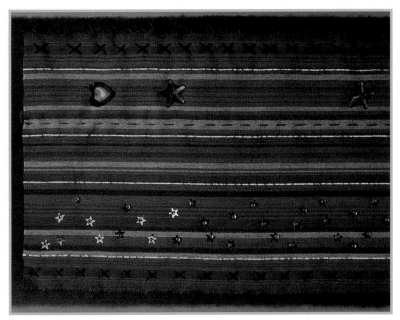

5 To make the channel for the ribbon handles, fold the short sides of the larger rectangle over the ends of the smaller rectangle. Pin in place.

4 Add more embroidery stitches to decorate the pink fabric and help secure it to the purple fabric. I have used pink running stitches that follow the stripes on the fabric. Add the craft jewels to the bag as shown, following the instructions for sewing on sequins on page 16.

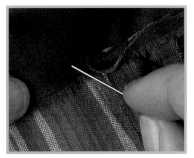

6 Sew the ribbon channel in place with small running stitches. Once this is done, repeat at the other end of the bag.

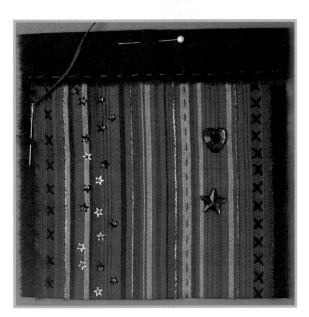

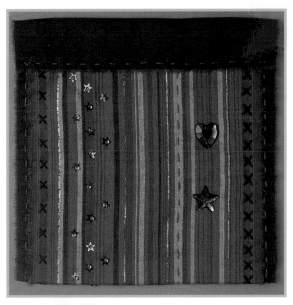

7 Fold the bag in half, by bringing the ribbon channels together, and pin in place. Use small running stitches to sew up the side but make sure that you keep the ribbon channels open at the top.

8 Start and finish this stitching carefully so that it is strong enough to hold the bag together. Repeat on the other side.

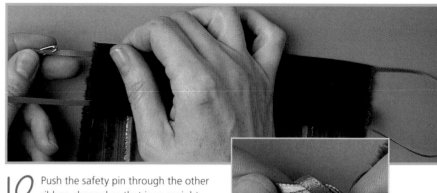

9 To add the ribbon handles, fix a safety pin to the purple ribbon. Thread the safety pin all the way through the ribbon channel.

10 Push the safety pin through the other ribbon channel so that is goes right round the bag. Remove the safety pin and tie the ends of the ribbon in a knot (see inset).

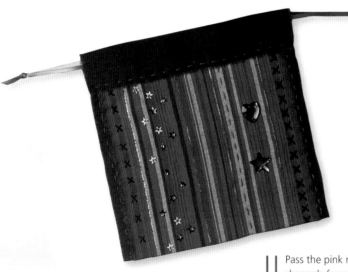

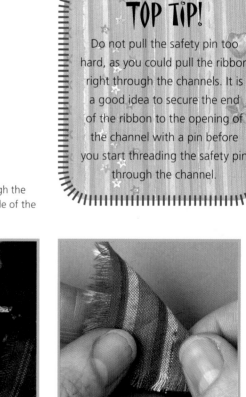

TOP TIP!

Do not pull the safety pin too hard, as you could pull the ribbon right through the channels. It is a good idea to secure the end of the ribbon to the opening of the channel with a pin before you start threading the safety pin through the channel.

11 Pass the pink ribbon through the channels from the other side of the bag and tie off as before.

12 Thread the tapestry needle with one length of the thick silver thread. Take the threaded needle through the lower edge of the ribbon channel as shown.

13 Pull the thread halfway through, remove the needle and tie the ends with a knot. Repeat with the other length of silver thread on the other side of the bag.

14 Take one of the small squares of fabric and fold it in half diagonally.

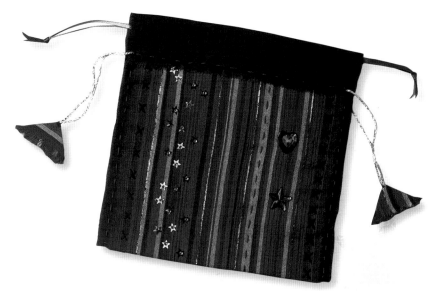

15 Fold the fabric in half diagonally again to form a smaller triangle. Wrap this around the knot on the silver thread, and attach the fabric to the knot with a small stitch.

16 Attach another square of fabric on the other side.

17 You can close the Magic Bag by pulling the coloured ribbons, and open it using the silver threads.

The finished Magic Bag is perfect for keeping treasures inside.

What next?

Use contrasting fabrics and couching to decorate the bag. Add decorations to all the handles.

Go mad with shiny fabrics and large sequins to make a gorgeous gift bag.

Make a large backpack with recycled denim. Decorate with frayed fabrics and buttons, then make the straps from strong cord.

FUNKY FACT!

This project was inspired by this small bag with two sets of drawstrings. The curved shape makes a circle when the handles are pulled shut.

Heart Purse

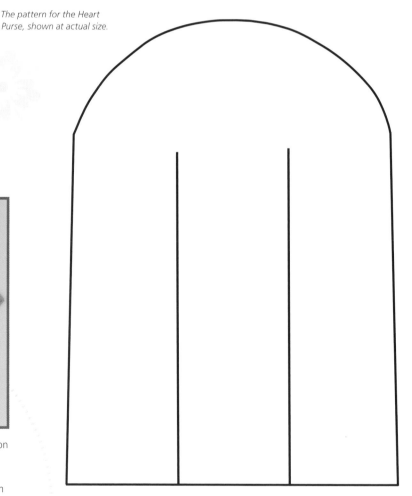

This heart-shaped purse is made from two pieces of folded felt woven together. The <u>weaving</u> is quick to do but the way that you decorate the purse is up to you. The decoration also holds the weaving together, stopping the fabrics from slipping apart. I have used mock sheesha, French knots and a heart button to fasten the purse.

The pattern for the Heart Purse, shown at actual size.

You will need

Tracing paper

HB pencil

Rectangles of blue and purple felt, each 24cm x 9cm (9½ x 3½in)

Large scissors

Embroidery needle

Pins

Purple stranded embroidery thread

Nine mock sheesha

One heart-shaped button

Narrow purple ribbon, 12cm (4¾in) long

1 Use the pencil to trace the pattern on to a sheet of tracing paper and cut it out. Fold the felt. Place the straight edge of the pattern on the fold and pin it in place.

Place this end on the fold in the felt.

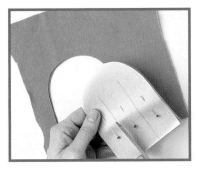

TOP TIP!

Try the weaving process with paper before you use felt so that you get used to the way of weaving the purse.

2 Use the scissors to cut around the pattern and along the lines as shown.

3 Repeat this process with the purple felt. The folded felt makes loops that are woven together to form the heart purse.

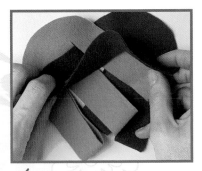

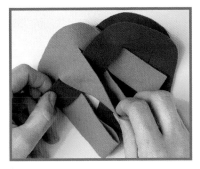

4 Begin to weave the purple felt into the blue felt as follows: Put the first blue loop through the first purple loop.

5 Put this purple loop through the second blue loop.

6 Put the third blue loop through the purple loop.

7 Now weave the second purple loop by putting it through the first blue loop.

8 Put the second blue loop through the second purple loop.

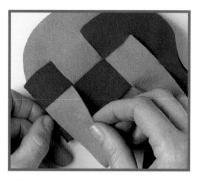

9 Put the second purple loop through the third blue loop.

10 Now weave the final purple loop by putting the first blue loop through it.

11 Put the third purple loop through the second blue loop.

12 Finally, the third blue loop goes through the third purple loop. Pull the purse into shape. You can open the purse because of the way the two side of the loops fit together.

TOP TIP!

Hold the purse open with your fingers while embroidering the decorations so that the two sides are not sewn together.

13 Sew the mock sheesha on to the purple squares of the weaving, following the instructions on page 19.

14 Stitch French knots into the blue squares, following instructions on page 15.

16 Add French knots and mock sheesha on to the back of the purse as shown.

15 Sew on the button at the top of the front of the purse.

17 Fold the ribbon in half. Sew it on with a small back stitch on the inside of the back of the purse. Make sure that you can fasten the purse by placing the ribbon over the button.

The finished Heart Purse.

41

What next?

Make a lovely shoulder bag by enlarging the pattern on a photocopier. For each side cut two pieces of each fabric and blanket stitch all of the edges before weaving. I have used denim and satin for the shoulder bag opposite. Decorate with jewels and embroidery stitches. Add buttons and ribbon loops to fasten and a long ribbon as a strap.

Weave red fabric together and embroider with cream running stitches along the edges.

Weave two pieces of denim together, with the pale side of one piece on the outside. Decorate with wavy lines of chain stitch.

Use two colours of felt and decorate with lots of buttons, then add cross stitches at each corner of the squares.

Lucky Charms

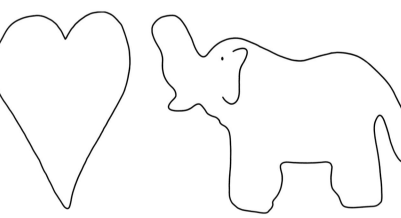

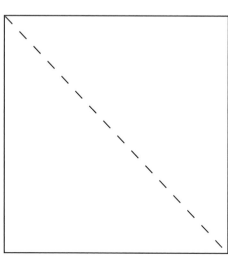

You will need

- Tracing paper
- HB pencil
- Grey felt
- Pins
- Large scissors
- Embroidery needle
- Pink and yellow stranded embroidery threads
- A selection of sequins and beads
- Polyester wadding (batting)
- Silver metallic thread

These embroidered felt charms are quick and easy to make. They use small amounts of felt so they do not cost too much. You can experiment with lots of ideas of your own and give them as presents to all of your friends and family.

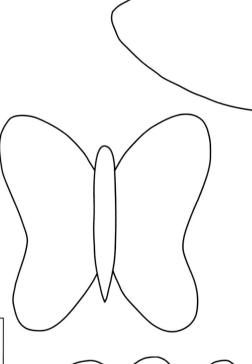

These patterns are reproduced at three quarters of their actual size. Enlarge them on a photocopier at 133 per cent for the correct size.

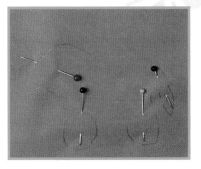

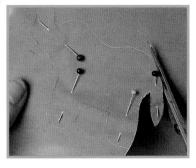

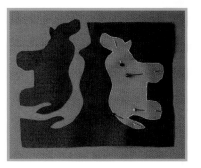

1 Trace the elephant pattern, and pin the tracing to the felt.

2 Cut out the elephant, and remove the pins.

3 Turn the elephant over and pin the tracing on to the felt again. Cut out the second elephant shape.

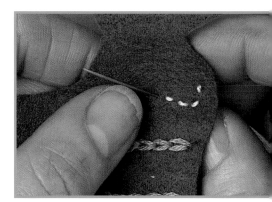

4 Decorate one side of the elephant with pink chain stitch lines. To make a more interesting end to the line, make a long stitch over the last chain loop as normal, but do not tie the thread off.

5 Take the thread back into the last loop of the chain, and make a second and third stitch to either side of the first stitch, as shown.

6 Use yellow stranded embroidery thread to mark the elephant's ear with a line of running stitch.

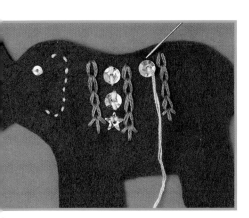

7 Sew sequins on to the elephant between the rows of chain stitch to build the design as shown. Sew on a small sequin as an eye.

8 Decorate the other side of the second elephant in the same way. Remember that it is important to get a pair of elephants facing each other so that the decorations remain on the outside when you sew the elephants together.

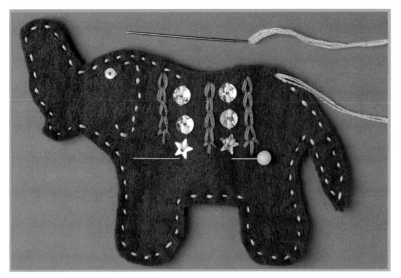

9 Put the two elephants together and pin. Sew with small running stitches near to the edge, but leave a small gap open at the top of the elephant.

10 Push a small amount of polyester wadding (batting) into the elephant to pad it out.

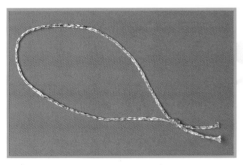

11 Make a loop by knotting the silver metallic thread as shown.

12 Place the knot into the gap at the top of the elephant and sew up the gap with running stitch.

The finished Lucky Charm.

What next?

Use the patterns on page 44 to make other lucky charms, and decorate them with buttons, beads, sequins and embroidery stitches. You could use a key ring fastening instead of the thread loop.

Heart: Use chain stitch and buttons.

Triangle: Start with a square of felt, decorate it and then fold it in half to make the triangle. The silver metal charms look good hanging off the shape.

Fish: This is decorated with spirals of running stitch and a heart-shaped sequin. It has a key ring fixed to it so you can use the charm to hold your keys.

Butterfly: Use fly stitch and sequins to show the markings of the butterfly.

Circle: Decorate with snowflake sequins and star jewels.

TOP TIP!

If you are using an asymmetrical shape, remember to turn the second side over so that you have two shapes that fit together.

More books to read

Traditional Indian Designs by Polly Pinder, Search Press, 2002
Chinese Designs by Elaine Hill, Search Press, 2003
The Embroidery Stitch Bible by Betty Barnden, Search Press, 2003
Embroidered Purses: Design and Techniques by Linda Tudor, Batsford, 2004
The Constance Howard Book of Stitches by Constance Howard, Batsford, 2005

A useful website

The Embroiderers' Guild has a very useful section for young embroiderers.
Their web address is: www.embroidersguild.com

Glossary

Couch To attach a thick thread to a piece of embroidery by overlaying it with thinner threads.

Skein A length of yarn, wound into a coil.

Sheesha A small mirror that is sewn on to a fabric. Sheesha are used a lot in Indian embroidery.

Translucent Partly see-through.

Weaving Interlacing threads or strips of fabric at right angles to each other.

Index

Start to...

An exciting new series packed with imaginative and irresistible projects for young people. Each book is brimming with ideas and techniques, with step-by-step photographs showing how to make funky bags and purses, trendy jewellery, fun wall hangings, belts, hats and much more. Enjoyable and entertaining, these books teach all the basic skills of knitting, quilting, embroidery and beading, while building up confidence. Discover how easy it is to create a whole range of beautiful items and learn how to embellish and personalise them with buttons, beads, sequins, ribbons and metallic threads.

Titles in this series

Start to Quilt
ISBN-10: 1-84448-109-3, ISBN-13: 978-1-84448-109-5

Start to Knit
ISBN-10: 1-84448-089-5, ISBN-13: 978-1-84448-089-0

Start to Bead
ISBN-10: 1-84448-131-X, ISBN-13: 978-1-84448-131-6

Start to Embroider
ISBN-10:1-84448-111-5, ISBN-13: 978-1-84448-111-8

About Search Press

- A huge selection of art and craft books, available from all good book shops and art and craft suppliers
- Clear instructions, many in step-by-step format
- All projects are tried and tested
- Full colour throughout
- Perfect for the enthusiast and the specialist alike
- Free colour catalogue
- Friendly, fast, efficient service
- Customers come back to us again and again

For the latest information on our books, or to order a free catalogue, visit our website: www.searchpress.com
Alternatively, write to us:
SEARCH PRESS LTD, Wellwood, North Farm Road, Tunbridge Wells, Kent TN2 3DR
Tel: (01892) 510850   Fax: (01892) 515903
E-mail: sales@searchpress.com

or if resident in the USA to:
SEARCH PRESS USA,
1388 Ross Street, Petaluma, CA 94954
Tel: (707) 762 3362   24 hour fax: (707) 762 0335
Email: searchpress@unicornbooks.com

Or if resident in Australia to:
SEARCH PRESS AUSTRALIA,
A division of Keith Ainsworth Pty Ltd,
Unit 6, 88 Batt Street Penrith 2750, NSW
Tel: 047 32 3411 Fax: 047 21 82 59
E-mail: sales@searchpress.com.au